1001

PELARGONIUMS

HAZEL KEY

1001

PELARGONIUMS

HAZEL KEY

B.T. BATSFORD · LONDON

A CIP catalogue record for this book is available
from the British Library.

ISBN 0 7134 8268 0

Printed in Spain

for the Publishers

B.T. Batsford
9 Blenheim Court
Brewery Road
London N7 9NT

A member of the Chrysalis Group plc

'Orange Parfait'
Orange flower with a white throat

CONTENTS

PELARGONIUMS: A BRIEF INTRODUCTION

Pelargoniums first appeared in Britain in the mid-seventeenth century. The species was collected in South Africa and brought to Britain in sailing ships from India, which called in at the Cape of Good Hope for food and water on the way back to England. In that first instance, it was wrongly recorded that these plants were collected in India itself.

Such voyages soon became regular trips to collect tea (which was increasingly in demand in Britain) and during this period over 200 species were brought back by way of seeds and plants to eagerly waiting gardeners and botanists. They first became popular amongst the wealthy who had the means to look after them, and because the species were so fertile, hybridisation took place easily.

Hundreds of cultivars were produced and within a century four distinct groups of hybrid pelargoniums started to circulate - they became the original ancestors of the hybrid cultivars we have here today. It is estimated that not more than twenty different species were used for their actual hybridisation, as many varieties were not compatible with each other. Four different groups formed, now known as Zonal, Regal, Scented Leaf and Ivy Leaf Pelargoniums – as well as sub groups such as Double Zonal, Fancy Leaf, Miniature, Dwarf, and Cactus types which developed by spontaneous sporting from these main groups. This stock has proved to be amply sufficient to provide enough variable genetic material to supply hundreds of different cultivars without repetition - and this process continues today.

By the early nineteenth century cultivars had already travelled to Europe, the USA, Australia and Canada, where they were eagerly welcomed by gardeners. Right from the beginning, these pelargonium cultivars had a commercial value, especially for the bedding plant trade. Because they put up a wonderful colourful display throughout the season, millions of pelargoniums are sold worldwide every year. It is a worthwhile trade for nurserymen and growers, who need to keep their stocks up to date and continue to produce new varieities in order to tempt customers.

A PELARGONIUM IS NOT A GERANIUM!

Following his in-depth studies on the genus *Pelargonium*, Prof. J. J. van der Walt, D.Sc., B.E.d credited the French botanist Charles Louis L'Heritier as its author in 1977. This was due to the fact that William Aiton had published Charles L'Heritier's unpublished manuscript, *Compendium Generalogum* in the first edition of *Hortus Kewensis* in 1792. Prof. van der Walt declared that these plants should, from that date onwards, be referred to as 'pelargoniums' and not 'geraniums' as the majority of gardeners had previously called them. Van der Walt's book has seemingly put an end to this error of names and people the world over are now in the process of learning to call a pelargonium a pelargonium. It certainly makes the genus easier to understand - both its past and what we can expect from it in the future. It must also help in improving breeding lines! Pelargonium species are required for this, and not geranium varieties – which are not physically related at all.

Hazel Key
National Pelargonium Collection
Pebworth
Warwickshire

PRIMARY HYBRIDS

Although very unusual in comparison to modern hybrids, these plants seem to have a great attraction for the present day gardener, even though they would not be used in the same way as the the modern pelargonium.

P. x 'Ardens' Green cut and serrated leaves and flowers on long stems held above the plant, which grow in clusters of wine-red, edged with light red. It is tuberous-rooted and is said to be a cross of *P. lobatum* and *P. fulgidum*.

P. x 'Schottii' Deep purple single flower held on tall stems which also carry serrated and cut leaves. Another *P. lobatum* and *P. fulgidum* cross.

P. x 'The Boar' Roundish lobed dark-green leaves with brown medallion in centre. Tall stems carry four narrow-petalled single salmon-pink flowers. Mass bloomer.

P. x 'Laurenceanum' Gouty looking stems support lobed leaves with serrated edges. Flowers grow on long stems in clusters of deep wine purple, edged pink. The flower also smells at night. A cross of *P. lobatum* and *P. fulgidum*.

P. x 'Scandens' Green leaves with dark green zone, single coral-red flowers on long stems. Prolific bloomer.

P. x 'Splendide' For nearly a couple of centuries this was considered to be a species but is now known to be a primary hybrid. Grey-green serrated sage-like leaves. Pansy-faced flower with purple upper petals and off-white lower petals. Needs to be grown with great care. Do not water too frequently.

REGAL PELARGONIUMS

Regal pelargoniums have trumpet-shaped six-petal florets growing in clusters and are some of the most beautiful cultivars in the whole pelargonium family. They make excellent house pot plants, and respond well to being grown in all types of containers, both inside and outside in the garden. They are not at their best grown in hanging baskets. The flowers come in a wide combination of colours and there are many named cultivars available to choose from. They are best grown from cuttings taken in the late autumn and rooted,

potted up and grown to flowering-pot size through the winter months in frost-free conditions. The low light and short day conditions actually help to grow a good plant without budding prematurely. They do not grow true to variety from seed. In reality, they are tender flowering shrubs, and given good growing conditions and regular feeds of high potash fertilizer, will bloom all spring and summer and on into the autumn, whilst long hours of daylight persist.

'Albert's Choice'
Clear orange-salmon flower, slight white throat, compact habit

'Alex Mary'
Mauve flower, white throat feathered purple

'Amethyst'
Deep lavender flower, blotched and feathered maroon

'Andrew Salvidge'
Purple and mauve flower, upper petals with pencil edge

'Angela'
Mauve flower, lightly feathered wine

'Ann Hoysted'
Deep crimson flower, upper petals almost black

'Ann Redington'
Mauve flower, purple upper petals

'Autumn Festival'
Orange-salmon flower, white throat

'Autumn Haze'
White overlaid salmon-rose flower, feathered
wine

'Antigua'
Red-pink flower overlaid burgundy-black, picotee edge on each petal

'Ashley Stephenson'
Creamy pink flower, bronze blaze on each petal

'Aztec'
Large pink flower, velvety brown markings on each petal

'Ben Matt'
Light claret flower, maroon on upper petals

'Beryl Reid'
Salmon-pink flower, overlaid brown and black

'Black Magic'
Black flower, dense habit

'Black Pearl'
Cerise-red, overlaid black

'Black Prince'
Black flower with pale pink picotee edge

'Blue Orchid'
Clear mauve flower, white throat

'Blush Mariquita'
White flower, red flash on upper petals

'Brandy'
Pale pink flower, blazed and feathered
burgundy

'Braque'
Deep rose-pink flower, upper petals blazed
mahogany

'Bredon'
Large wine-red flower

'Bronze Velvet'
Bronze red flower with darker blotches

'Brown's Butterfly'
Black flower, flecked mahogany and pink

'Burgundy'
Wine-red flower, compact plant

'Carisbrooke'
Large rose-pink flower, some maroon
markings on upper petals

'Cezanne'
White flower, upper petals purple

'Caprice'
Red-pink flower

'Chelvey'
Pale mauve flower, feathered wine

'Cherry Orchard'
Cherry-red flower with white throat

'Chew Magna'
White flower, blotched and veined sienna-red

'Chiquita'
Large rose-pink flower

'Chorus Girl'
Lavender-blotched salmon flower, ruffled margin

'Colonial Boy'
Brick-red flower, wine throat

'Circus Day'
Large carmine flower with purple splashes

'Clown'
Flushed white flower, blazed and feathered wine

'Confetti'
Lilac and mauve flower, purple marks on petals

'Conspicuous'
Wine-red flower, overlaid deep purple

'Country Girl'
Candy-pink flower with strawberry markings

'Covina'
White flower, upper petals blazed deep purple

'Dark Presido'
Rose-pink flower, upper petals purple-black

'Dark Secret'
Deep mahogany flower, feathered burgundy

'Dark Venus'
Almost black flower

'Delilah'
Rose-pink flower, upper petals mahogany

'Delli'
Pinky-mauve flower and white, frilly edge

'Destiny'
Pure white flower

'Doris Frith'
White flower with wine feathering on upper petals

'Doreen Featherby'
Purple-black and pink flower

'Doris Shaw'
Large mauve flower, with violet marks on
each petal

'Dubonnet'
Wine-red flower, feathered deep purple

'Dunkery Beacon'
Fiery orange flower, lightly feathered plum

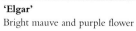

'Eileen Postle'
Wine-red flower, edged light lavender with
dark burgundy blaze

'Elgar'
Bright mauve and purple flower

'Elfin Rapture'
Soft apricot flowers, short bushy plant

'Elsie Hickman'
Pink flower, edged maroon, white throat

'Elizabeth Taylor'
Pink and white flower, wine-red blaze on upper petals

'Enid Blakeby'
Orange flower, overlaid red

'Fareham'
Purple and lilac flower, picotee edge

'Fascination'
Rose-pink flower, dark crimson markings

'Fanny Eden'
Orange-salmon flower on white background

'Field Marshall von Mackeson'
Red-pink flower, feathered deep wine

'Fifth Avenue'
Purple-black flower

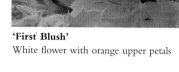

'First Blush'
White flower with orange upper petals

'Flair'
Palest pink flower, lightly feathered wine

'Fleur d'Amour'
Frilly pale pink flower, white throat

'Fringed Aztec'
Pink flower, brown marks on fringed petals

'Geoffrey Horseman'
Mauve flower, feathered deepest purple

'Gentle Georgia'
Pale apricot-pink flower

'Georgia'
Soft salmon flower, upper petals mahogany

'Georgia Peach'
Soft mid-peach-pink flower

'Georgina Blythe'
Pale pink flower, veined purple; white throat

'Glensheree'
Carmine-salmon flower; upper petals feathered red

'Gloria Pearce'
Deep rose-pink flower, feathered garnet

'Goldie'
Light orange flower, white throat, wavy petal

'Gordano Midnight'
Dark mahogany flower, almost black, on short bushy plant

'Grenada'
Coral-salmon and white bi-coloured flower

'Grossmutter Fischer'
Orange flower, dark blotch on each petal

'Harewood Slam'
Cherry-red flower, with dark wine-red
markings

'Happy Valley'
Ruffled pink flower, veined red

'Hazel'
Large violet-purple flowers, compact habit

'Hazel Cherry'
Red-pink flower with with mahogany blaze

'Helena Hall'
Light scarlet flower, blazed mahogany

'Honeywood Hannah'
Mallow-purple flower, feathered crimson

'Honeywood Jonathan'
Salmon-pink flower, mahogany upper petals

'Horace Parsons'
White flower with crimson blaze on each petal

'House and Garden'
Red and white flower with dark purple upper petals

'Howard Stanton'
Mauve flower, white throat and maroon feathering on upper petals

'Humanist'
Pink and white flower with wine-red blaze

'Jim Field'
Purple-black flower

'Julie Smith'
Lavender and purple flower

'Kaufman's Bonfire'
Purple-pink flower, overlaid scarlet, blazed and
feathered purple-black

'Joan Fairman'
White flower, flushed pink and blotched maroon

'Joy'
Beautifully frilled salmon-pink and white flower

'Kamahl'
Frilly pink petals, white throat and wine-coloured upper petals

'Lachlan Piers'
Large salmon flower with burgundy blaze on upper petals

'Lamorna'
Cerise-scarlet flower, pink throat feathered wine

'Langley'
Red-pink flower, white throat, feathered deep wine

'La Paloma'
Large white flower, faintly marked purple

'Lara Waltz'
Lilac-pink flower, frilly petals, feathered wine

'Laurel Hayward'
Deep burgundy flower, blazed dark purple

'Lavender Grand Slam'
Mauve flower with wine blaze on upper petals

'Lavender Sensation'
Frilly lavender-pink flower with plum markings

'Leslie Judd'
Shell-pink flower, feathered red

'Lilac Domino'
Pinky-mauve flower

'Lord Bute'
Purple-black flower, edged wine

'Lowood'
Purple-mauve flower with deep purple markings

'Lustre'
Ruffled orange-salmon flower

'Love Song'
Pink flower, upper petals overlaid deep purple, under petals veined red. Cream and green variegated leaves

'Luz del Dio'
Pale salmon-pink flower, blazed burgundy

'Magic Moments'
Large salmon flower with orange-white throat

'Magnum'
Lavender flower, blotched and feathered cerise

'Marchioness of Bute'
Almost black flower, edged purple, petals crimped making flower look double

'Mahogany'
Light burgundy-red flower

'Margaret Salvidge'
White flower, overlaid wine-red; blazed and
feathered deepest purple-black

'Margaret Soley'
Purple and mauve flowers

'Margaret Thorpe'
Orange-scarlet flower with orange blotch on
upper petals

'Margaret Waite'
Red flower, shaded orange and salmon

'Marie Rober'
Large violet flower, shaded purple

'Marie Vogel'
Light red flower with dark blotches on upper petals

'Mariquita'
Salmon-pink flower, feathered burgundy

'Melanie'
Purple flower, white throat feathered wine; petals edged pink

'Melissa'
Salmon-pink flower

'May Magic'
Salmon-orange flower, white throat

'Meon Maid'
Crimson-black-red flower

'Mere Cocktail'
Light purple flower, blazed magenta on each petal

'Mere Flamenco'
Light wine-red flower, heavily blazed deeper wine

'Mere Meteor'
Mahogany-wine flower

'Mere Sunglow'
Soft salmon-orange flower

'Mexicali Rose'
Cerise-pink flower, white throat, darker upper petals

'Minstrel Boy'
Deep mahogany-black flower

'Miss Australia'
Pink flower with silver leaf

'Modigliani'
Mauve flower, blazed deepest purple

'Mohawk'
White and coral-pink flower with dotted red
border

'Mme Thibault'
Coral-pink and white bi-coloured flower

'Mollie'
Scarlet flower, overlaid crimson

'Mona Larkin'
Coral-pink flower, white throat, upper petals
blotched burgundy

'Mood Indigo'
Mauve-pink flower, blazed deepest wine

'Moonflight'
Rosy-cerise flower, red-purple markings

'Morello'
Mahogany flower, blazed wine

'Morwenna'
Deep purple-black flower

'Morf's Red'
Light wine flower

'Mrs G Morf'
Purplish-mauve flower, ruffled

'Maja'
Pink flower, upper petals blotched crimson

'Nancy Hiden'
Rose-pink flower, blotched wine; white throat

'Naunton Velvet'
Palest pink flower, overlaid burgundy

'Music Man'
Red-pink flower, blazed burgundy on each petal

'Navajo'
Vivid rose flower, lightening towards edge

'Nelly'
Pink flower, burgundy blaze on top petal

'Neuhuit C. Fass'
Mauve flower, purple blaze on each petal

'Noche'
Deep mahogany flower, edged coral-red

'Orange Parfait'
Orange flower with a white throat

'Ostergruss' syn. 'Easter Greetings'
Cerise-pink flower, each petal blotched black

'Pamela Underwood'
White flower, wine-red pencilling on some petals

'Pax'
Pale pink flower, upper petals heavily blazed wine

'Pat Thorpe'
Soft pink flower, blazed and feathered purple

'Peggy Sue'
Deep magenta flower, overlaid black-beige on each petal

'Phyllis Mary'
Light crimson flower, white throat

'Phyllis Richardson'
Double rose-pink flower

'Pink Bonanza'
Large pale salmon flower, white throat

'Pink Slam'
Salmon-pink flower

'Pink Margaret Pearce'
Pink flower, blotched maroon; white throat

'Primavera'
Rose-pink and white flower, frilly

'Princess Josephine'
Light purple flower with black blaze and
feathering

'Princess of Wales'
Strawberry-pink flower, white crimped edges
and white centre

'Prof. Eckman'
Pink flower, white throat, upper petals deep
purple

'Purple Emperor'
Lavender flower, feathered crimson-purple

'Quantock'
Orange-salmon flower, blotched on upper petals

'Rapture'
Soft peach-pink flower

'Red Velvet'
Deep crimson flower, overlaid wine

'Rhodamine'
Mauve and white flower, blazed wine

'Rimfire'
Black flower with scarlet edge

'Rita Coughlin'
Pale lavender flower

'Robbie Hare'
Soft salmon flower deepening to orange-salmon

'Rogue'
Large mahogany-crimson flower, shading to black

'Rosmaroy'
Lilac-pink flower, frilled

'Salmon Slam'
Deep salmon flower, wine feathering on upper petals

'Sefton'
Cerise-red flower, overlaid deep wine, feathered and blazed

'South American Bronze'
Bronze flower with white pencil edge

'Solano'
Orange flower, feathered burgundy and white

'Senorita'
Salmon-red flower, upper petals stained mahogany

'Special Moment'
Light crimson flower, overlaid with purple
blaze

'Strawberry Sundae'
Bright strawberry-pink flower, clear white
centre

'Sunrise'
Large orange-salmon flower with white throat

'Ted Dutton'
Orange-salmon flower with white throat

'Valencia'
Orange-scarlet flower with burgundy
feathering on upper petals

'Sybil Bradshaw'
Violet flower, overlaid purple on upper petals,
feathered black

'Valenciana'
Salmon-pink flower, feathered burgundy

'Verity Pallas'
Mahogany-purple flower, pale pink throat

'Vicky Clair'
Deep red flower, edged violet, lower petals
white and veined crimson

'Vicky Town'
Pale mauve flower, overlaid mahogany on each petal

'Victoria Regina'
White flower with a burgundy blaze on each petal

'Violetta'
Deep purple flower, blazed and feathered purple-black

'Wellington'
Orange-coral flower with white throat and upper petals blazed mahogany

'Virginia'
Frilled pink flower, lower petals lavender

'White Glory'
White flower

'William Sutton'
Pink flower, overlaid scarlet, maroon blaze

'Wookey'
Cherry-red flower, upper petals flushed
salmon-orange and with black blotches

'Yhu'
Pale pink flower, overlaid wine, feathered
purple-black

'Zulu King'
Light crimson flower, overlaid purple-black, feathered wine

ANGEL PELARGONIUMS

Angel pelargoniums are small-leafed, flowering plants which grow on long stems and have a bushy habit. There are two types grown under the one name; the originals which were raised round about 1825, parents unknown, and the modern type which were first raised in the 1930s by a gardener called Langley Smith. This modern type had one of its parents as *P. crispum*, thus giving these plants their small flowers and foliage. Derek Clifford, scholar, nurseryman and researcher of pelargoniums in the late 1940s and 50s, wrote a highly factual book on these plants. He believed that the two groups should be amalgamated as they were similar, and that they should all be called by the same name, Angels. With hindsight this was not a good idea, as they are two entirely different types of plants and not of the same breeding lines, and to the frustration of many gardeners since, they can not be made to hybridize freely. The original Angels did not have scented leaves, so any development has been due to *P. crispum* hybrids, and over the years this side of the group has expanded somewhat. The plants are very fine in hanging baskets if allowed to trail - though some people prefer to stop them very hard and have tight little bushes of flowers. By letting them grow in their own fashion they certainly have more flowers, and are longer-lasting, outstandingly lovely and very eye catching.

'Androcles'
Pale mauve flower, feathered and blazed wine on the upper petals

'Baby Snooks'
Lavender-pink flower, upper petals blotched purple

'Bouquet Centre'
White flower with purple feathering on upper petals

'Catford Belle'
Mauve ruffled flower with purple upper petals

'Culm'
Pale lavender-pink flower, upper petals purple with pink picotee edge

'Fairy Orchid'
White flower with purple blotches on upper petals

'Fringed Angel'
Pale pink flower, upper wavy petals blotched ruby

'Gosbeck'
Pale lavender flower, purple blaze on upper petals

'Grace'
Mauve flower, purple blaze on upper petals

'Jer'rey'
Deep velvet purple flower, red-pink picotee edge

'Kettlebaston'
Mauve-pink flower, top petals purple

'Mrs G. H Smith'
White flower, light purple blaze on upper petals

'Little Blakenham'
Pale lilac flower with red blotches on upper
petals

'Mole'
Purple and white flower petals

'Moon Maiden'
Lilac flower with purple spot on upper petals

'Needham Market'
Pale mauve flower, feathered purple

'Raspberry Ripple'
Pink flower with upper petals deeper pink

'Rita Scheen'
Pale pink flower, upper petals blazed wine,
variegated gold and green foliage

'Neil Cleminson'
Purple-pink flower with ruby blaze on upper two petals

'Rose Bengal'
Mauve-pink flower with upper petals purple

'Swedish Angel'
White flower, two upper petals purple, lower petals half-purple with white throat

'Southern Belle'
Pink flower, upper two petals blazed and feathered ruby

'Veronica Contreras'
Lavender flower with large purple blotch on each petal

'Zoe'
Pale pink flower, upper petals blotched wine and feathered on lower petals

UNIQUE PELARGONIUMS

Unique pelargoniums are a very old group which have been around since the beginning of the nineteenth century. Research shows that they were trialed by the Royal Horticultural Society at their Chiswick trial grounds in 1860 to determine their value as bedding plants. They did not perform well and were given a second chance in 1861 – yet still did not produce good results.

Having grown them ourselves at Fibrex Nurseries for 45 years, I think that the soil conditons then were probably too nitroginous for them. Since growing them in a compost high in potash and regularly feeding them with a high potash feed, we have always produced marvellous plants, full of bloom and long-lasting, and I can now understand why they were well regarded. The fact that they are still around – though for years were not thought much of – is a credit to their durability, and that alone should be recommendation enough. If they are dealt with correctly they are also beautiful, floriferous and easy to grow.

'Aurore's Unique'
Light-green lobed leaf, upright habit; red flower, blotched and feathered wine

'Bolero' (Raised in U.S.A.)
Pink flower, blazed wine. Regal-type leaf

'Carefree' (Raised in U.S.A.)
Red-pink flower. Regal-type leaf

'Claret Rock Unique'
Claret-red flower. Tall grower. Regal-type leaf

'Crimson Unique'
Large deep crimson flower with black markings on all petals. Pointed Regal-type leaf

'Hula' (Raised in USA)
Single salmon-pink flower, dark feathering, with a shallow-lobed leaf

'Jessel's Unique' syn. 'Mrs Kingsbury'
Purple flower, wavy lobed leaf

'Key's Unique'
Salmon-pink flower, darker upper petals with deepest wine centre and feathering. Regal-type leaf

'Mme Nonin'
Mauve, pink and white flower, cut and divided blunt leaves

'Mons Ninon'
Attractive crimson and pink, ruffled and crimped flower. Leaves cut and well divided

'Paton's Unique'
Lovely deep crimson-shaded pink flower with maroon veins

'Mystery' (Raised in U.S.A.)
Deep wine flower, blotched black

'Phyllis'
Cream to yellow and green, variegated form of 'Paton's Unique'

'Pink Aurore's'
Pink flower with darker blotch. Large cut Regal-type leaf

'Polka' (Raised in U.S.A.)
Orange-red flower, blotched and feathered deep purple

'Robins Unique'
Scarlet flower. Low and slow growing plant. Very free flowering

'Rollers. Satinique' (Raised in U.S.A.)
Salmon-pink flower, deeply cut grey-green
foliage

'Scarlet Unique' syn. 'Mrs Taylor'
Showy bright scarlet flower. Free-growing
shrubby plant. Pungent scent

'Violet Unique'
Violet flower. Sport from 'Scarlet Unique'.
Very eye catching

'Rollinson's Unique'
Bright purple-red flower, lobed leaf

'White Unique'
Free-flowering, glistening white flower on dense foliage

SCENTED-LEAF PELARGONIUMS

Scented-Leaf pelargoniums seem always to have been around. Many of the early species that came to England in the eighteenth century had scented leaves, so that the hybrids produced in the early days for flowering plants had distinctive foliage that was also scented with many different perfumes. They became popular for these attributes alone, the flower often secondary in importance.

Many cultivars were named and lost in the first 250 years but we now have around 100–150 named cultivars which belong solely to the scented leaf section. These are pelargoniums with attractive leaves which have agreeable, interesting and pleasant perfumes and make good plants for the house and/or garden. Many people are still not aware of this group of plants' existence and are surprised and delighted when seeing them for the first time. They propagate easily from cuttings in the same manner as other pelargoniums, and can be grown as decorative pot plants inside, or in the garden as feature plants. Lining a garden path, they give off a very evocactive perfume when brushed against. The leaves can be used as flavouring in cakes and apple jelly and also for scenting pot-pourri.

They bloom in the spring and early summer, usually with small flowers – but as they are grown chiefly for their foliage and perfume, and not for their flowers which do not smell – it does not seem to matter too much. However, if Scented-Leaf pelargoniums are fed regularly with high potash tomato feed, they will improve their performance greatly in terms of quantity and quality of bloom.

'Andersonii'
Dark zoned leaf, mallow-purple flower with dark purple marks. Pungent

'Apple Betty'
Apple loft scent, rounded tri-lobed leaf. White flower

'Ardwick Cinnamon'
Grey-green leaf, cinnamon scent. White flower

'Aroma'
Pleasant sweet fragrance of apples; grey-green, small rounded leaf. White flower

'Atomic Snowflake'
Tri-lobed leaf, blotched and striped creamy
white. White flower. Pungent

'Blandfordianum Roseum'
Deeply cut grey-green leaf. Small rose-pink
flowers

'Attar of Roses'
Tri-lobed rounded rose-scented leaf. Mauve flower

'Both's Snowflake'
Deeply divided mottled green and white leaf,
lemon-rose scent. Pink flower

'Brilliantine'
Round leaf with *eau de cologne* scent. Small
purple flower

'Brunswick'
Large leaf, strongly perfumed oak-leaf type.
Coral flower

'Camphor Rose'
Deeply cut and lobed leaf, with camphor
scent. Light purple flower

'Candy Dancer'
Light mauve-pink flower with deeply cut
rose-scented leaf

'Capri'
Red and pink flower, deeply cut lobed leaf

'Charity'
Cut and lobed medium-sized yellow-green variegated leaf with citrus scent. Mauve flower

'Charmay Snowflurry'
Lemon balm scent, tri-lobed green and cream-
blotched leaf. Mauve flower

'Chocolate Peppermint'
Tri-lobed leaf, dark brown mark down centre.
Mauve flower. Peppermint scented

'Citriodorum'
Round grey-green leaf, mauve flower, musky
citrus scent

'Citronella'
Small rough palmate leaf; bushy upright habit,
strong citrus scent. Mauve flower

'Clorinda'
Cedar-scented, tri-lobed leaf. Large rose-pink flower. Tall grower

'Concolour Lace'
Small cut filbert, nut-scented, small rose-red
flower, overall leaf

'Copthorne'
Lobed leaf, large mauve flower, very sweetly
scented

'Crispum Major'
Mid-green crinkled leaf with lemon scent.
Upright form with pale mauve flower

Crispum 'Minor'
Small crinkled leaves, mauve flower, upright habit

Crispum 'Variegatum'
Attractive cream and green variegated leaf, lemon scent

'Crowfoot Rose'
Grey-gresen foliage. Rose-scented lavender flower

'Dark Lady'
Large, grey-green leaf, peppermint scent. Mauve flower

'Endsleigh'
Tri-lobed leaf, attractive salmon-pink flower. Smells of *P. fulgidum*

'Dean's Delight'
Deeply-cut sticky grey-green leaf. Mauve flower. Pungent

'Fillicifolium'
Fern-like foliage, balsam-scented, pale mauve flower. Selected fine form of *P. denticulatum*

'Fair Ellen'
Dark oak-shaped leaf with spicy scent; compact growth. Pretty mauve flower

'Fragrans'
Grey-green foliage, white flower, pine scent

'Frensham'
Rough rounded serrated leaf with strong citrus scent. Mauve flower

'Fruity'
Round leaf, bushy habit, fruit-pine scent. White flower

'Galway Star'
Green and cream variegated leaf, lemon scent. Pale mauve flower

'Gemstone'
Small lobed leaf, sweet fruity scent. Pretty mauve and purple flower

'Giant Oak'
Large oak-leaf shaped leaf, clusters of purple-mauve flowers, strong turpentine scent

'Golden Clorinda'
Gold and green form of 'Clorinda'. Bright pink flower

'Golden Well Sweep'
Gold variegated form of *P. crispum*. Tiny lemon scented leaf with mauve flowers

'Grace Thomas'
Large pointed grey-green leaf with sweet citrus scent. Pale mauve flower

'Graveolens of Hort'
Cut, lemon-rose scented leaf. Mauve flower

'Green Lady'
Large round leaf with peppermint scent.
White flower

'Grey Lady Plymouth'
Silver-grey leaf, rose-lemon scent. Mauve
flower

'Hermanus Show'
Cut peppermint-scented leaf. Strong growing
hybrid of S. African origin

'Islington Peppermint'
Hybrid between *P. tomentosum* and *P. 'Splendide'*. Small flower, black upper petals, white lower
petals. Peppermint-scented leaf

'Jello'
Small slender leaves with strawberry-jelly
scent. Mauve-pink flower

'Joy Lucille'
Peppermint scent, deeply cut leaf. Small pale
mauve flower, marked with darker purple

'Karooense'
Cut green lobed leaf, with strong medicated scent. Mauve flower

'Lady Plymouth'
Cream and green variegated form of Graveolens. Small pale rose flowers, veined purple

'Lady Scarborough'
Sweet lemon-rose scented leaf. Pink flower, veined purple

'Lara Jester'
Deeply cut leaf, spicy rose scent. Mauve-pink flower with white eye

'Lara Starshine'
Pale green deeply cut fine leaf with spicy sharp scent. Red-pink flower

'Lemonair'
Roundish serrated lemon-scented leaf, bushy habit. Mauve flower

'Limoneum'
Small rounded leaf, sweet lime-rose scent.
Mauve flower

'Lemon Fancy'
Rough textured, serrated leaf, citrus scent. Mauve flower

'Little Gem'
Cut lobed green leaf with rosy-lemon scent.
Mauve flower. Short bushy habit

'Mabel Grey'
Rough deeply-cut leaf; strong lemon scent.
Mauve and purple flower

'Maple Leaf'
Rough maple-leaf shaped, pungent-scented,
large leaf with mauve flower

'Marie Thomas'
Very fragrant round leaf with pale mauve
flower

'Nervous Mabel'
Round slightly crimped leaf with lemon
scent. Mauve flower

'Olga Shipston'
Round notched leaf, odoratissimum-type
seedling. White flower

'Orange Fizz'
Heavily orange-scented, coarse, lobed leaf with purplish flower

'Orchid Clorinda'
Mauve sport of rose pink 'Clorinda'

'Paloma Oak'
Green serrated leaves. Mauve flower with
serrated petals. Oily, fruity smell

'Peach Cream'
Small round green and cream leaf, erratic
variegations, lemon scent. Mauve flower

'Peter's Luck'
Lobed divided leaf with strong citrus scent.
Mauve flower

'Pink Capricorn'
Shallow tri-lobed, lemon-rose scented leaf.
Mauve-pink flowers with a white eye

'Pink Champagne'
Round grey-green leaf, lemon scent. Cerise-pink and mauve flower. Upright habit

'Pink Paradox'
Small somewhat round leaves, fringed at edges.
Small mauve dainty starlight flower. Sweet
smelling

'Pretty Polly'
Light green oak-leaf shaped leaves. Pink flower
with wine blotched on upper petals. Ginger
mint smell

'Princeanum'
White flower with purple blaze on upper
petals. In shady positions, this flower changes
colour to pale mauve. Orange scent. (Called
'Orange' in USA)

'Radula'
Straight, narrowly pointed lobes on deeply-cut
rough leaf, rose-lemon scent. Pale purple flower

'Prince of Orange'
Round pointed leaf, orange scent. Pale mauve flower. Bushy habit. (Not the same as 'Princeanum')

'Radula Rosea'
Deeply cut fan-shaped leaf, oily rose smell.
Rose-red flower

'Rober's Lemon Rose'
Grey-green blunt, sagitate leaf; rose-lemon
scent. Mauve flower

'Round Leaf Rose'
Large sprawly plant, rounded medium-sized leaves. Mauve flowers. Lemon-rose scent

'Shrubland Rose'
Mildly scented, tri-lobed leaf. Pretty rose-pink flower

'Sweet Lady Mary'
Small round leaf, deep mauve upper petals, paler lower petals, lemon-scented. Like original 'Lady Mary' but with strong perfume and stiffer growth habit

'Royal Oak'
Dark green, oak-leaf shaped leaf with central dark blotch. Turpentine scent. Mauve-purple flower

'Sarah Jane'
Lobed leaf, lilac flower with strong citrus scent

'Secret Love'
Divided cut leaf, eucalyptus scent. Mauve flower

'Sweet Mimosa'
Deeply-cut lobed leaf with sweet scent. Large pink flower

'Torrento'
Smooth, green, ginger-scented, tooth-edged leaf. Mauve flower

'Sweet Rosina'
Large grey-green graveolens-type leaf. Strong citrus and rose scent

'Variegated Fragrans'
Pine scent, white and cream variegated leaf, small tri-lobular indented leaves

'Welling'
Large red-pink flower with lobed leaf, faintly scented

'Afterglow'
Single pale pink flower, darker centre

SINGLE ZONAL PELARGONIUMS

All single zonals have five-petalled flowers which are naturally arranged in a regular pattern of two petals up and three down below. The hybridist's ideal is for large, flat and round flowers, with petals arranged regularly (not overlapping) and no space showing between the petals, held on strong stems which are not too long. Single zonal pelargoniums appeared, in the first instance, as a result of the crossing of the two species, *P. zonale* and *P. inquinans*, and these two plants are regarded as the earliest ancestors.

'Ainsdale Claret'
Single purple-red flower

'Ainsdale Eyeful'
Single scarlet flower with white eye

'Amarantha'
Single coral-rose flower

'Ashfield Serenade'
Single pale lavender-pink flower

'Beauty'
Single scarlet-cerise flower

'Belvedere Glory'
Single bright cerise-pink flower

'Bliss'
Single coral-pink and white flower

'Cleopatra'
Single pale lavender-pink flower, white centre

'Christopher Ley'
Single orange-scarlet flower, white eye

'Cramden Red'
Single scarlet flower

'Dale Queen'
Single soft salmon-pink flower

'Dawn Flush'
Single light salmon flower

'Deerwood So Big'
Single white flower, dashed and dotted light red

'Doris Moore'
Single cherry-red flower

'Dream'
Single white and pale pink flower

'Dublin'
Single rose-flushed scarlet flower

'Edmund Hockey'
Single salmon flower

'Elizabeth Angus'
Single salmon-scarlet flower with white eye

'Feurrisse'
Huge, single crimson flower

'Elizabeth Cartwright'
Single crimson-scarlet flower

'First Love'
Single pale pink flower, deeper red at centre

'Flowerfield'
Single red flower, white centre

'Focus'
Single orange-scarlet flower, white eye

'Francis James'
Single pale pink flower, light crimson centre

'Gaudy'
Single, magenta overlaid red flower

'Freckles'
Single pink flower, cerise dot on each petal

'Gilbert West'
Single magenta flower, white eye

'Harvest Moon'
Single orange flower, white eye

'Harvey'
Single, magenta overlaid scarlet flower

'Highfield's Symphony'
Single pink flower, shaded salmon

'Honne Frueling'
Single pale pink flower, deeper centre

'Immaculata'
Single white flower

'Hope'
Single cerise-red and white bi-coloured flower

'Iron Duke'
Single large soldier-tunic-red flower

'Jeanne'
Single fringed flower, petals shades of pink.
(This is not the same as Skelly's Pride)

'Josephine'
Single large coral-red and white bi-colour
flower

'Kingswood'
Single coral-red and white flower

'L. E. Warton'
Single pink flower with white eye

'La Fiesta'
Single large scarlet flower

'Lady of Spain'
Single pale coral-pink and white flower

'Lilian Woodbury'
Single cerise-pink flower, small white eye

'Maloja'
Single orange-scarlet flower

'Mary Seaton'
Single scarlet flower, white centre

'Maxim Kovalevski'
Single orange flower

'Mere Casino'
Single red flower with light stripes all over
surface of flower

'Mme Dubarry'
Single pale cerise-red flower

'Mrs Cannel'
Single pale salmon flower, white centre

'Nellie Nuttal'
Single pale salmon-pink flower

'Nottinghill Beauty'
Single salmon flower

'Nouvelle Aurore'
Single apricot-pink and white flower

'Nuit Poteviene'
Large, single red-purple flower, orange splash
in centre

'Onalee'
Single fuchsia-pink flower, white eye

'Paul Crampel'
Single scarlet flower

'Perfect'
Single light crimson flower, small white eye

'Persian Rose'
Large, single cerise-purple-pink flower

'Phyllis'
Single coral-salmon flower

'San Sovino'
Single orange-scarlet flower

'Salmon New Life'
Single flower, salmon-pink, splashed with white

'Sonne Sport'
Single magenta flower with crimson dash on each petal

'Snowstorm'
Single white flower

'Springfield Glory'
Single pale salmon and white bi-colour flower

'Staplegrove Fancy'
Single white flower, spotted and striped coral

'Stadtbern'
Single dark scarlet flower

'Sparkle'
Single white flower, edged and flushed carmine

'Starburst'
Single pink flower, striped red

'Tom Tit'
Single small pink floret which grows in small clusters

'Vera Dillon'
Single purple-red flower, scarlet on upper petals

'Xenia Field'
Single pale pink flower, light scarlet centre

'Willie Kolle'
Single mauve-pink flower, white eye, dark dots

'Winston Churchill'
Large, single, deep crimson flower, white eye

'Yvonne'
Single white flower, edged and marked cerise-pink

'Alex Kitson'
Semi-double, creamy lavender-pink flower

DOUBLE AND SEMI-DOUBLE ZONALS

Double and semi-double zonals developed from spontaneous sporting on the early single zonals in France in the latter half of the nineteenth century. Three different forms appeared. One is a double-type zonal like a rosebud. Another is a double with petals all over the flower itself, but containing not more than twenty petals in all. There is also a semi-double form with a somewhat 'cup and saucer' effect to each floret. This produced the largest bloom of all. These were soon being used by hybridizers, and before long many of the cultivars were being produced worldwide. It was quickly realised that these double-flowered plants make very good pot plants, as well as garden plants if the weather conditions are good. Since then thousands of different doubles have been produced. A general consensus of opinion is that double cultivars are superior to the single cultivars, and are therefore more appealing to the pelargonium fancier.

'A M Mayne'
Double magenta flower, scarlet centre

'Ange Davey'
Semi-double rose-pink flower

'Alys Collins' A.G.M.
Double pale pink flower

'Ashfield Monarch'
Semi-double red flower

'Audrey'
Double rose-pink flower

'Astrachan'
Double dark wine flower

'Autumn'
Double orange flower

'Ballerina'
Double orange-red flower

'Baronne A. de Rothschild'
Semi-double pale lilac-pink flower

'Beauty of El Segundo'
Double soft creamy-pink flower

'Beryl Gibbons'
Semi-double white, flushed palest-pink flower

'Beatrix'
Double purple-red flower, scarlet on upper petals

'Black Country Bugle'
Double carmine-pink and white bi-coloured flower

'Blossomtime'
Semi-double salmon-rose-pink flower

'Bold Sunset'
Semi-double light pink, flushed salmon flower

'Brenda Kitson'
Semi-double rose-pink flower, white base
upper petals

'Carol Gibbons'
Semi-double white flower

'Bonanza'
Double light carmine-pink flower

'Chelsea Morning'
Semi-double flushed white flower, large wine
dots on lower petals

'Colonel Drabbe'
Double crimson flower with small white eye

'Cotswold Queen'
Semi-double palest peach flower

'Credo'
Semi-double light crimson flower, overlaid scarlet

'Dagata'
Semi-double mauve flower with a white eye

'Creamery'
Double pale yellow flower

'Decorator'
Semi-double orange-red flower

'Dr Mary Sturgess'
Semi-double coral-pink flower, large white centre

'Dr Miroslav Tyrs'
Double salmon-pink flower

'Double Jacoby'
Double crimson-scarlet flower

'Duke of Buckingham'
Semi-double orange-scarlet flower

'Eric Ellis'
Double biscuit-pink flower

'Dodd's Super Double'
Double large salmon-red flower

'Downlands'
Semi-double pale salmon flower, deeper salmon in centre

'Esteem'
Semi-double coral-salmon flower

'Evesham Wonder'
Semi-double salmon-pink flower

'Fiat'
Semi-double coral-salmon flower

'Fortune'
Double white flower, flecked salmon-pink
(bird's egg type)

'Frau Kathe Neubronner'
Double light purple flower, white centre

'Garibaldi'
Double pale creamy salmon flower

'Geoffrey Harvey'
Semi-double crimson flower

'Garnet'
Double dark wine-red flower

'Genetrix'
Semi-double coral-rose flower

'Glenn Barker'
Double shocking pink flower, upper petals
based white

'Glory'
Double orange flower

'Gracious Lady'
Semi-double white flower, flushed pale pink

'Graefin Mariza'
Semi-double coral-pink flower

'Gustav Emich'
Semi-double bright scarlet flower

'Gypsy'
Double crimson-purple flower, white centre

'Halloween'
Double orange flower, white eye

'Hanchen Anders'
Semi-double cerise-pink flower

'Hannah Brook'
Double magenta-pink flower, white eye

'Hans Rigler'
Semi-double brilliant scarlet flower

'Highfield's Attracta'
Semi-double palest pink flower, edged and
shaded salmon

'Hermoine'
Double pure white flower

'Highfield's Sugar Candy'
Double white flower, flushed palest pink

'Hildegarde'
Semi-double orange-scarlet flower

'Improved Ricard'
Semi-double orange-scarlet flower

'Inspiration'
Semi-double palest pink flower

'Jacqueline'
Semi-double scarlet flower

'Janet Hofman'
Semi-double salmon-pink flower

'Jean Oberle'
Semi-double palest pink flower

'Jewel'
Double carmine-pink flower

'Kath Peat'
Double pale salmon-pink flower, deeper
centre

'King of Denmark'
Semi-double salmon-pink flower, based white

'Lady Ilchester'
Double silvery-pink flower

'Kenny's Double'
Double bright rose-red flower

'Lavender Bird's Egg'
Double lavender-pink flower, spotted on all
petals

'Lavender Ricard'
Semi-double purple rose flower, white eye

'Layton's White'
Double white flower

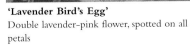

'Le Lutin'
Double cerise-red flower, white eye

'Lorelei'
Double pale salmon-pink flower

'Magda'
Double pale pink flower, overlaid red dots and splashes

'Marktbeherrscher'
Semi-double rose-carmine flower with darker markings

'Loripen'
Semi-double coral-red flower

'Memories'
Semi-double lavender-pink flower

'Millie'
Semi-double scarlet-orange flower

'Melva Bird'
Double crimson flower

'Mme Thibault'
Double purple-pink flower, each petal white based

'Mrs Chaplin'
Double purple flower with white eye

'Mrs Lawrence'
Double flesh-pink flower

'Mrs Tarrant'
Double palest salmon-pink flower, darker edge

'Nell Smith'
Semi-double bright coral-salmon flower

'Orange Ricard'
Semi-double orange flower

'Obergartner Held'
Semi-double purple-pink flower, white base to
upper petals

'Olympia'
Semi-double neon-pink flower

'Orangesonne'
Double orange flower

'Paisley Red'
Semi-double red flower

'Patience'
Double purple-pink flower, white centre

'Paul Humphries'
Semi-double deep crimson flower

'Pink Pearl'
Double palest pink flower, white centre

'Pink Bouquet'
Semi-double creamy pink flower

'Pink Raspail'
Double lavender-pink flower

'Reflections'
Double orange flower

'Regina'
Double pale pink flower, overlaid salmon

'Rosemine'
Semi-double rose-pink flower

'Rubin'
Semi-double scarlet-red flower

'Rotleib'
Double orange-red flower

'Rubella'
Double scarlet and white picotee-edged
flower

'Ryecroft Pride'
Double crimson flower

'Santa Maria'
Semi-double deep salmon-pink flower

'Stanton Drew'
Semi-double salmon-pink flower

'Sophie Koniger'
Semi-double coral-pink flower

'Summer Cloud'
Semi-double white flower

'The Speaker'
Semi-double fiery salmon flower

'Trautleib'
Semi-double phlox-pink, dwarf habit flower

'Treasure'
Double pale salmon-peach flower

'Tresor'
Double white, striped and flecked salmon-pink flower

'Triomphe de Nancy'
Double flower of an unusual shade of light purple

'William Tell'
Double dark purple flower

'Vivat Regina'
Semi-double creamy, pale pink flower, deeper centre

'Zinc'
Double profuse scarlet flowers on compact low growing plant

DEACONS

This strain of double zonal pelargoniums was raised by the late Rev. S. P. Stringer of Norfolk whose hobby was plant breeding, especially pelargoniums. He produced many new cultivars from the late sixties onwards and this particular range of double zonals proved to be very popular. They were even on the show bench then, although they were smaller flowered than the semi-double types such as the Irenes. These plants come in a wide range of colours and have a very bushy habit after the growing tips have been pinched out a time or two. The name 'Deacon' covers many seperately named plants. Nurseries listed them as a group and gardeners bought them as such; it was unwittingly an exercise in 'increased sales', although it becomes awkward for nomenclature.

'Deacon Barbecue'
Double claret-rose flower

'Deacon Constancy'
Double pale rose-pink flower

'Deacon Coral Reef'
Double salmon-coloured flower

'Deacon Fireball'
Double scarlet flower

'Deacon Manderin'
Double bright orange flower

'Deacon Minuet'
Double two-tone pink flower

'Deacon Moonlight'
Double pale mauve flower

'Deacon Lilac Mist'
Double pale lavender-pink flower

IRENE ZONAL PELARGONIUMS (AMERICAN)

Irenes should really be listed under doubles and semi-doubles, but they have always been referred to as a separate group, especially in Britain. The difference between them and other semi-doubles is not really obvious at first glance, but in England they have qualities which set them apart, in that they can be grown easily in soil-less composts - unlike many varieities that preceded them. They are easy to grow through the winter months at low temperatures and under poor light conditions, and they propagate without difficulty. As well as making good bedding and pot plants, Irenes bloom early, thereby making a sellable plant in the very early spring which is of course ideal for the general nursery trade.

'Cal'
Semi-double salmon-pink flower

'Electra'
Semi-double crimson-red flower

'Genie'
Semi-double salmon-rose flower

'Irene'
Semi-double crimson-red flower

'Modesty'
Semi-double white flower

'Party Dress'
Semi-double pale mauve flower

'Penny'
Semi-double fuchsia-pink flower with large
white eye

'Rose Irene'
Semi-Double rose-pink flower

'Springtime'
Semi-double light salmon flower

'Warrior'
Semi-double scarlet flower

PELFI/PAC PELARGONIUMS

Two particular strains of zonal pelargoniums are the Pelfi zonals and Pac zonals. These popular varieties were bred commercially in Germany at the nurseries of Gerhard Fischer and Wilhelm Elsner respectively, and are subject to plant breeders' rights. Thus they cannot be propagated commercially without royalties being payable to the raisers. For the Pelfi varieties, rights are owned by Fischer, Am Scheid, D-56204 Hillscheid, Germany. For the Pac varieties, rights are owned by Elsner Pac, Jungpflanzen, Dresden, Germany.

Pelfi 'Disco'
Semi-double cerise-red flower

Pelfi 'Dolce Vitae'
Semi-double pale salmon flower

Pelfi 'Gloria'
Semi-double orange flower

Pelfi 'Madison'
Semi-double shaded-salmon flower

Pelfi 'Rokoko'
Semi-double salmon flower

Pelfi 'Tango'
Semi-double dark red flower

Pelfi 'Twist'
Semi-double salmon-scarlet flower

Pelfi 'Volcano'
Semi-double scarlet flower

Pac 'Bruni'
Semi-double crimson flower, compact
bushy habit

Pac 'Ice Crystal'
Semi-double lavender flower, upper petals
purple and white, purple dots on lower petals

Pac 'Lachsball'
Semi-double salmon-pink flower

Pac 'Lovesong'
Semi-double pink flower with crimson dots
on each petal

Pac 'Penve'
Semi-double magenta-purple flower

Pac 'Perlenkette Orange'
Semi-double orange flower

Pac 'Rosepen'
Semi-double cerise-pink flower

Pac 'Sassa'
Semi-double cerise-pink flower

FANCY-LEAF ZONAL PELARGONIUMS

This section is grown chiefly for its remarkably handsome foliage. In fact, in Victorian times, the flowers were often removed (they were small and single) when they were bedded out. Whilst the original silver-leaf, gold-leaf and bronze-leaf forms all originated by mutation, the tri-colour forms were the result of hybridization between bronze-leaf and silver-leaf types, which resulted in these almost artifical-looking colours and markings. It is remarkable that we still have as many of these varieties as we do in current circulation. They were first hybridized by Peter Grieve chiefly. These pelargoniums are not at all easy to grow and I think this is because of the current practice of using soil-less compost. Whether it is the fertiliser in the compost or the peat itself that causes the trouble, I am not sure. But in the days when Fancy-Leaf Zonals were first raised, the formula for growing them was loam, a little dried cow manure, grit and sometimes leaf mould. The plants would probably last several seasons in this type of compost.

Today's raisers, who are producing even lovelier varieties with double flowers, advise that the plants need to be renewed each year and not grown on. However one thing is certain - you need to be fairly skilled to grow them well. The tri-colours are also slow-growing and take a long time to grow back again after they have been used for cuttings. In fact, if you are using soiless compost, do not cut the plants back too severely or they will not recover. Avoid taking cuttings in the winter. The best time is mid-summer, when there is plenty of light.

'A Happy Thought'
Single light crimson flower

'Albert Sheppard'
Double cerise-red flower, green-gold leaf, bronze zone

'Ben Franklin'
Double pink flower, silver leaf

'Betwixt'
Single red flower, green-silver, pointed ivy-like
tri-coloured leaf

'Bewerley Park'
Double salmon-pink flower, black bronze leaf

'Blazonry'
Single cream and red bi-coloured flower

'Bristol'
Single bright scarlet flower, gold tri-colour
foliage

'Butterfly Lorelei'
Double soft salmon flower, dark green leaf,
yellow-green butterfly central zone

'Camely'
Double red flower, wavy bronze zone, gold
leaf

'Cherry Cocktail'
Double red flower, gold tri-colour foliage

'Chelsea Gem'
Double pale pink flower, white centre, silver
leaf, short grower

'Cherie Bidwell'
Double salmon-red flower, silver tri-colour
foliage

'Caroline Schmidt'
Double crimson-red flower, silver leaf, good
bedding cultivar

'Cherie Maid'
Single palest pink flower, salmon eye, silver
foliage

'Cherry Sundae'
Double cerise flower, silver foliage

'Deacon Peacock'
Double orange-scarlet flower, gold centred,
with bronze zones

'Contrast'
Single scarlet flower, golden tri-colour foliage

'Display'
Single salmon-pink flower, golden tri-colour
foliage

'Distinction'
Single scarlet flower, dark green leaf with
narrow black ring near centre edge of leaf,
serrated

'Dollar Princess'
Single scarlet flower, tri-colour leaf

'Dolly Varden'
Single scarlet flower, tri-colour leaf

'Don's Carousel'
Single red flower, tri-colour foliage

'Don's Mona Nobel'
Single scarlet flower, gold tri-colour foliage

'Don's Silver Pearl'
Single orange-scarlet flower, golden tri-colour foliage

'Fair Maiden'
Single cerise flower, silver leaf

'Filgree'
Single salmon flower, cream, green and red tri-colour foliage, dwarf habit

'Falklands Hero'
Single red flower, golden tri-colour foliage

'Flower of Spring'
Single scarlet flower, silver leaf

'Frank Headley'
Single salmon-pink flower, silver leaf

'Freak of Nature'
Single vermilion flower; white stem and stalk, green-edged white leaf

'Freda Warden'
Single bright pink flower, narrow black ring around dark green edge, serrated leaf

'Frosty'
Single mauve flower, green, cream and bronze leaf

'Gold Crest'
Single salmon-pink flower, green-gold leaf with bronze zone

'Harold Headley'
Single rose-pink flower, green-gold leaf with
bronze zone

'Greetings'
Single salmon flower, silver tri-colour foliage

'Helter Skelter'
Single red flower, green and cream tri-colour
foliage

'Hills of Snow'
Single pink flower, silver leaf

'Henri Jonquet'
Double cherry-red flower, silver foliage

'Jungle Leaf'
Single red flower, green leaf with light
butterfly centre and rust-red zone

'Lin Davis'
Double delicate blushed white flower, yellow
leaf with bronze zone

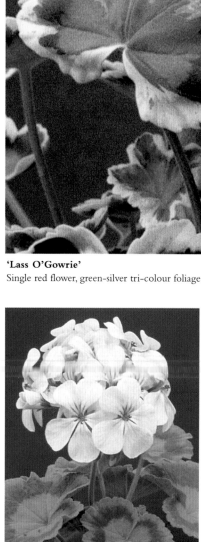

'Lass O'Gowrie'
Single red flower, green-silver tri-colour foliage

'Little Margaret'
Single scarlet flower, cream and golden tri-
colour foliage

'Love Storey'
Pale pink flower, chocolate zone, green-gold
leaf

'Lucy Gunnet'
Double cerise flower, tri-colour foliage

'Mac's Red'
Single red flower, bronze zone on gold leaf

'Mangles Variegated'
Single red flower, pale green leaf with deeper green butterfly in centre

'Magic Lantern'
Single salmon flower, gold–green leaf with dark bronze zone

'Mary Spink'
Double salmon-pink flower, gold leaf, bronze zone

'Master Paul'
Double palest pink flower, silver leaf

'Milden'
Single pale pink flower, spotted and splashed scarlet

'Mavis Colley'
Single salmon flower, cream and golden tri-colour foliage

'Miss Burdette Coutts'
Single red flower, scarlet, cream and gold tri-colour foliage

'Mme Butterfly'
Single red flower, silver leaf

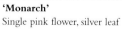

'Monarch'
Single pink flower, silver leaf

'Mont Blanc'
Single white flower, silver leaf

'Moor'
Double red flower, green leaf with dark brown medallion

'Mrs Farren'
Single red flower, cream and green tri-colour foliage

'Mrs Mappin'
Single white flower with pink centre, silver leaf

'Mr Henry Cox'
Single pale pink flower, golden tri-colour foliage

'Mrs Parker'
Double deep rose-pink flower, silver leaf

'Mrs Pollock'
Single orange flower, golden tri-colour foliage

'Mrs Strang'
Double orange flower, golden tri-colour foliage

'Occold Embers'
Double salmon flower, overlaid pink, green
and gold foliage

'Occold Volcano'
Double bright red flower, gold foliage, bronze
zone

'Mrs Quilter'
Single pink flower with gold leaf, bronze zone

'Pink Dolly Varden'
Single pink flower, cream tri-colour foliage

'Platinum'
Single salmon flower, silver leaf

'Preston Park'
Single salmon flower, green scalloped leaf
edged with thin black zone

'Princess Alexandra'
Double pink flower, silver leaf

'Pygmalion'
Double red flower, green-gold leaf with wide
irregular bronze zone

'Ray Coughlin'
Double orange flower, dark brown medallion
on green leaf

'Rene Roue'
Double red flower, silver foliage

'Royal Sovereign'
Double red flower, gold leaf, bronze zone

'Richard Key'
Double pale mauve flower, green-gold leaf with bronzed wavy zone

'Sophie Dumaresque'
Single red flower, golden tri-colour leaf

'Silver Wings'
Single silvery-pink flower, silver leaf

'Scarlet Pimpernel'
Single red flower, golden tri-colour foliage

'Silver Ruby'
Double crimson flower, silver leaf

'Silver S. A. Nutt'
Double crimson flower, silver leaf

'Sussex Beauty'
Salmon-red flower, silver foliage

'Violet Lambton'
Single violet flower, bronze, yellow and green leaf

'Turkish Delight'
Single orange flower, green, gold and bronze leaf

'Turtle's Surprise'
Double red flowers, white stems; green, gold and bronze zoned leaf with light gold centre

'Ursula Key'
Double coral-salmon flower, golden leaf with chestnut zone

'Wycombe Lodge'
Double cerise-red flower, green-gold leaf with bronze

'Wantirna'
Single scarlet flower, green leaf with cobweb markings

'Wirral Target'
Single salmon flower, cream tri-colour foliage

'Wirral Sunset'
Double salmon flower, gold tri-colour foliage

'Wirral Moonglow'
Double salmon flower, tri-colour foliage

CACTUS ZONAL PELARGONIUMS

This sub-group of zonal pelargoniums developed by spontaneous mutation from single and double zonal types, beginning in the mid-nineteenth century. They were so named because they look like the quilled petals of cactus flowering dahlias, and not because they were bred from the succulent cactus-type species of pelargonium. The flowers are quite interesting as novelty plants but would not make much of a show as bedding plants. Sports still appear randomly, and some of the plants we already have produce further sports in different colours to the same cultivars.

'Attraction'
Double salmon-red flower

'Brockbury Scarlet'
Single scarlet flower

'Cherry'
Double coral-red flower

'Coralina'
Double rose-pink flower

'Fascination'
Double pale salmon-pink flower with white centre

'Hulda Conn'
Double coral-salmon flower

'Pink Poinsettia'
Double lilac-pink flower with white eye

'Spitfire'
Double scarlet flower, silver leaf

'Star of Persia'
Double light cerise-pink flower

'Tangerine'
Double orange flower

'Noel'
Double white flower

ROSEBUD ZONAL PELARGONIUMS

DOUBLE FLOWERS RESEMBLING
TIGHT RAMBLING ROSEBUDS

The rosebud pelargonium sub-group was one of the first double pelargonium types. They appeared by spontaneous mutation in the pelargonium zonal cultivar around 1850 and were much sought after in Victorian times for buttonholes and posies. Rosebud pelargoniums are very difficult to hybridize because the florets are so tightly held in the flower: the stamens and styles are not very accessible and they produce little if any pollen. This is the reason that this section is not very large.

They are best used as pot plants under glass, as the bloom damps easily if rained or watered upon.

'Appleblossom Rosebud'
Double white and red flower, bi-colour

'Gladys Evelyn'
Double coral-red flower

'Le Febre'
Double brick-red flower

'Noele Gordon'
Double rose-pink flower

'Pink Rambler'
Double pale pink flower

'Plum Rambler'
Double deep claret flower

'Red Rambler'
Double brick-red flower

STELLAR ZONAL PELARGONIUMS

FIVE-FINGERED ZONAL PELARGONIUMS

Stellars are flowers with unusually shaped petals and leaves. They originally came from Australia and were bred from a plant called the Chinese Cactus. This was not a species but had great potential as a parent plant; many different cultivars were raised from it, and indeed still are worldwide. It is another example of the potential pelargoniums carry in their genes to intrigue and delight us.

'Ade's Elf'
Single coral-pink flower, white eye

'Arctic Star'
Single white flower

'Alan West'
Single pale salmon flower with white upper petals

'Apricot'
Single light orange flower

'Bali Sunrise'
Single blended coral-salmon and pink flower

'Bird Dancer'
Single spidery pale salmon flower, mass
bloomer

'Cathay'
Single pale pink flower

'Deerwood Pink Puff'
Double pale pink flower

'Dawn Star'
Single salmon flower

'Easter Morning'
Single coral-pink flower, white upper petals

'Fandango'
Single salmon flower

'Golden Ears'
Single light scarlet flower, bronze leaf

'Golden Staph'
Single orange-red flower, gold leaf with
bronze zone

'Green Ears'
Single salmon-pink flower, bronze zoned leaf

'Grenadier'
Double scarlet flower

'Hannaford Star'
Single deep salmon flower, white eye

'Helen Christine'
Single magenta flower, dwarf habit

'Letitia'
Single pale salmon flower

'Judy Swinbourne'
Double salmon flower

'Meadowside Dark and Dainty'
Single small salmon flower

'Meadowside Harvest'
Single deep salmon flower, bronze leaf

'Morning Star'
Single white flower

'Pagoda'
Double white and pink flower

'Persimmon'
Single coral-pink flower

'Meadowside Midnight'
Single orange flower, almost black leaf

'Pixie Prince'
Double shaded salmon and white flower

'Pixie Rose'
Double rose-red flower, small white eye

'Prim'
Double white flower

'Rad's Star'
Single pink flower, upper petals half white, bi-coloured

'Ragtime'
Semi-double orange-scarlet flower

'Purple Heart'
Single red flower, almost black leaf

'Raspberry Sweet'
Double cerise-red flower

'Red Demon'
Single scarlet flower

'Ruth Lesley'
Single white flower

'Solent Star'
Single orange flower, flushed gold leaf

'Satellite'
Single salmon flower

'Staccato'
Single mid-scarlet flower, some white on
upper petals

'Startel Red'
Single red flower

'Startel Salmon'
Single salmon flower with white eye

'Sunraysia'
Single dark salmon-coral flower

'Tracery'
Single white flower, red eye

'Vancouver Centennial'
Single salmon flower with dark brown
medallion on yellow leaf

'White Feathers'
Double pink-flushed white flower

'Super Nova'
Double lilac-pink flower, narrow and frilly

'Vectis Glitters'
Single white spotted and splashed-pink flower

'Vectis Gold'
Single salmon flower with white eye and gold leaf

MINIATURE ZONAL PELARGONIUMS

These charming little plants which are perfectly formed - though every part is miniature - should only measure 13cm (5") high from the top of the soil in the pot to the top of the foliage in a 9cm (3 1/2") pot. Blooms can be taller than the plant, but must be in proportion. If the plant grows bigger, it should be classified as a Dwarf. Obviously, if it is potted it will grow taller and wider, but will still retain its miniature form. These measurements are the limits allowed for an exhibition plant. Miniature zonal pelargoniums propagate easily, though it is advisable to avoid damping off by propagating them in the late spring. This ensures that they are well-grown before the autumn and winter arrive. Water very carefully and sparsely in winter, trying not to wet the plant itself. They are rather vulnerable to damping off in the early stages because they are so near the soil. These plants bloom profusely and make very good window-sill plants as they do not take much space or grow too high, and are ideal for the housebound gardener.

'Adele'
Double pink flower, upper petals white based

'Aerosol'
Single mauve flower with wine birds-egg speckling, green leaves

'Ailsa'
Double white flower

'Ambrose'
Double white flower

'Andromeda'
Single palest pink flower, salmon centre

'Anna'
Single cerise-pink flower

'Anne Screen'
Single pale mauve flower

'Arizona'
Double pink-purple flower, upper petals based
white

'Aries'
Single orange-salmon flower

'Baby Brocade'
Double white flushed coral-pink flower

'Baby Birdsegg'
Single pale pink flower, pale purple spots, green leaf

'Bantam'
Double salmon-orange flower

'Beatrice'
Single cherry-red flower

'Belinda Adams'
Double off-white flower, overlaid salmon

'Berylette'
Double light salmon flower

'Betsy Trotwood'
Single pale lavender flower, white base to
upper petals

'Black Knight'
Single scarlet flower, black foliage

'Blush Kleiner Leibling'
Very small, single pale pink flower in clusters

'Brenda Hyatt'
Semi-double magenta-pink flower, with white
eye

'Brookside Primrose'
Double pale salmon flower, light yellow-green
foliage

'Brightwell'
Double rose-pink flower, green leaf

'Burnaby'
Double salmon-pink flower

'Capricorn'
Double pink flower

'Caligula'
Double scarlet flower, black leaf

'Celia'
Single pale pink flower, white eye

'Chelsworth'
Double orange-salmon flower

'Cheiko'
Double light wine-red flower

'Cherie'
Single deep coral-red flower, white based
upper petals

'Cherry'
Single scarlet and white bi-colour flower,
green leaf

'Clair'
Single pale rose-pink flower, upper petals
based white

'Coral Frills'
Double salmon-pink quilled petalled flower,
dark foliage

'Codenham'
Double orange-red flower

'Crestwood Pink'
Single bright pink flower

'Crowfield'
Double lavender-pink flower, small white eye

'Davinia'
Double shaded salmon-pink flower

'Cupid'
Double carmine-pink flower, black leaf

'Denebola'
Double palest pink flower

'Dianne'
Double dawn-pink flower with paler shading

'Didi'
Single salmon-pink flower

'Dinky'
Double light red flower

'Dolly Read'
Single pale pink flower, darker centre, white eye, black leaf

'Dolphin'
Single coral-pink and white bi-colour flower

'Dwarf Miriam Baisey'
Single scarlet and white bi-colour flower

'Eden Gem'
Double cerise-pink flower

'Embassy'
Single scarlet flower, small white eye

'Etna'
Single scarlet flower, dark leaf

'Escapade'
Semi-double soft-salmon flower

'Fairy Tales'
Single creamy-white flower, flushed pale pink

'Firelight'
Single vivid scarlet flower, black leaf

'Fleurette'
Double salmon-rose flower

'Francis Parrett'
Double light purple flower

'Frills'
Double pale salmon-pink flower

'Gladys Stevens'
Double purple flower

'Geoff May'
Single coral-salmon and white bi-coloured flower

'Goblin'
Double scarlet flower

'Golden Princess'
Single orange flower, white centre

'Grace Wells'
Single fuchsine-pink flower

'Grenadier'
Single vermilion flower

'Grey Sprite'
Single coral-salmon flower with dull silver leaf

'Heidi'
Double pale pink flower, deepening to rose-pink on edge and centre

'Hitcham'
Double bright scarlet flower

'Jane Eyre'
Double mauve-pink flower

'Janet Kerrigan'
Double pale pink flower, deeper centre

'Jaunty'
Double carmine-red and white bi-coloured flower

'Jupiter'
Double crimson-scarlet flower

'Kerensa'
Double white flowers edged cherry-red

'Kesgrave'
Double salmon-pink flower

'Krista'
Double red flower

'Kyra'
Double white flower, lightly flushed pink

'Levington'
Double salmon-pink flower

'Lenore'
Double apricot-orange flower, white centre

'Little John'
Double salmon-pink flower, paler at edges

'Liza'
Single pale pink flower, darker centre, white
eye

'Lyric'
Double lavender-pink flower, white centre

'Madge Hall'
Single carmine-pink deepening to red, and
white bi-coloured flower

'Margery Stimpson'
Double lavender-pink flower, white centre

'Martin Parrett'
Semi-double mauve flower, white eye

'Marmalade'
Double salmon-orange flower

'Medley'
Semi-double large white flower

'Memento'
Double light salmon-apricot flower

'Milbourne Clover'
Double clover-pink flower, dark foliage

'Nancy Grey'
Single pale pink flower, white eye and coral-
pink ring

'Minx'
Double deep wine flower, dark foliage

'Nicor Star'
Single white flower with pink star in centre

'Orange River'
Double orange flower

'Orion'
Double orange-scarlet flower

'Pauline'
Semi-double light carmine-pink flower

'Peace'
Single large salmon-pink flower, black leaf

'Phyllis Read'
Single coral-red and white bi-colour flower

'Pink Fondant'
Double palest pink flower

'Pixie'
Single coral-salmon flower

'Prince Valiant'
Single wine-red flower

'Rebecca'
Semi-double light carmine flower

'Red Spider'
Single orange-scarlet flower

'Red Black Vesuvius'
Single scarlet flower, black leaf

'Redondo'
Double scarlet flower, black leaf

'Rigel'
Double scarlet flower, black leaf

'Rose Beauty'
Double rose-red flower

'Ruby'
Double carmine-red and white bi-coloured
flower

'Salmon Vesuvius'
Single pale salmon-pink flower

'Rushmere
Double salmon-pink flower

'Sasha'
Single orange-salmon flower

'Shenandoah'
Single shocking pink flower

'Silver Kewense'
Single crimson flower, narrow petals

'Sleurings Robin'
Double scarlet flower

'Snowdon'
Single white flower, centre flushed pink

'Snowbaby'
Double white flower, green leaf

'Sunspot Kleine Liebling'
Single pink flower, yellow foliage with green
butterfly zone

'Telstar'
Double light cerise-scarlet flower

'Tiberius'
Single light cerise-red flower

'Twinkle'
Double rosy-salmon flower

'Trinket'
Double soft salmon flower

'Variegated Petit Pierre'
Single pink flower, silver leaf. (Sported in Great
Britain, different from 'Variegated Kleiner Leibling')

'Venus'
Double pale pink flower

'Variegated Kleiner Liebling'
Single pink flower, gold and green leaf (Sported in USA)

'Wycombe Maid'
Double creamy-pink flower, salmon centre

'Wensum'
Double salmon-pink flower

'White Roc'
Double white flower, flushed pink

'Wallis Friesdorf'
Single scarlet narrow-petalled flower

'Witnesham'
Double pale salmon-pink flower

DWARF PELARGONIUMS

These plants grow larger than Minatures and their size is classed at 20cm (8") high from soil level to the top of the plant, grown in 4 $^1/_2$" (11 $^1/_2$ cm) pots. They make lovely bushy plants, ideal for window boxes or on the window-sill, and are very floriferous and rewarding for the housebound gardener.

'Angelique'
Double crimson overlaid scarlet flower

'Ada Sutterby'
Double cerise-pink flower, rosebud type

'Annabelle Stephenson'
Double scarlet flower

'Barnston Dale'
Double cerise-pink flower

'Ben Nevis'
Double white flower

'Betty Kite'
Double rose-pink flower

'Beryl Reid'
Double salmon-pink flower

'Bidleston'
Single orange-pink flower, splashed and
spotted red on all petals

'Blushing Emma'
Double pale pink and white flower

'Brackenwood'
Double pink flower

'Bridesmaid'
Double pale pink flower

'Bright Eyes'
Single deep pink flower

'Brookside Jupiter'
Single salmon flower with white eye

'Brookside Serenade'
Single lavender-pink flower with white eye

'Brookside Astral'
Double pink flower

'Cameo'
Double deep pink flower, white eye

'Chatisham'
Single cream flower with red vein centre, gold and bronze leaf

'Clatterbridge'
Double red flower

'China Doll'
Double light salmon flower, paler at edges

'Cindy'
Double pale pink flower

'Constance'
Double rose-pink flower

'David John'
Single white flower

'Daydream'
Double salmon-pink flower, gold leaf, bronze zone

'Dresden White'
Single white flower

'Dresden Pink'
Single salmon-rose flower, narrow petals

'Elmsett'
Double pale pink flower, spotted and dashed red with gold leaf

'Elizabeth Read'
Single fuchsia-pink flower, white splashes

'Emma Hossler'
Double mauve-pink flower

'Enid Read'
Single cerise-red flower

'Fantasia'
Double white flower

'Emma Jane Read'
Double lavender-pink flower

'Fenton Farm'
Single purple flower, white eye with gold leaf

'Friesdorf'
Single scarlet flower, narrow petals

'Goldust'
Bushy with green edged gold leaf, salmon
flower

'Henhurst Gleam'
Double cerise-scarlet flower

'Holbrook'
Double salmon-pink flower with gold leaf

'Honeywood Suzanne'
Semi-double pale pink flower

'Lanham Royal'
Double ruby-rose-pink flower

'Leith Hill'
Double white flower

'Little Alice'
Double salmon-rose flower

'Michelle'
Single salmon-pink flower with small white
eye

'Little Fi-Fine'
Single salmon flower with gold leaf

'Monsal Dale'
Double strawberry-pink flower, gold leaf

'Morning Cloud'
Double pale salmon flower

'Morval'
Double china-pink flower

'Mr Everaarts'
Double shocking pink flower

'Nadine'
Double soft salmon flower

'Occold Profusion'
Semi-double pale pink flower

'Peace Palace'
Single rose-pink flower

'Nettlestead'
Double peach-pink flower

'Penny Serenade'
Single brilliant mandarin-red flower

'Petite Blanche'
Double white flower crowned with pink flush

'Pink Lively Lady'
Single pink flower with gold leaf

'Pot Pourri'
Double palest pink flower

'Powder Puff'
Double salmon flower

'Ragamuffin'
Double pink flower

'Rosina Read'
Double pale salmon flowers

'Samantha Stamp'
Double pale pink flower with gold leaf

'Salmon Beauty'
Double salmon-crimson flower

'Shirley Anne'
Double rose-pink flower

'Spital Dam'
Double pale pink flower

'Stella Reid'
Single soft pale pink flower, darker centre and edge

'Sunrocket'
Double orange flower

'Surprise'
Double palest pink flower

'Susan Payne'
Double pink flower

'Trudy'
Single soft mauve-pink flower, narrow petals

'Tammy'
Double deep coral-red flower

'Tutone'
Double pale pink flower

'Wallis Friesdorf'
Double red flower

'White Lively Lady'
Single white flower with gold leaf

'Zena'
Single white flower, speckled and splashed
with violet

'Wendy Read'
Double salmon-rose flower

IVY-LEAF PELARGONIUMS

These cultivars have a naturally trailing habit and so lend themselves to any position where their trailing form can enhance the situation, such as in hanging baskets, tubs and window boxes. It would be no exaggeration to say that millions of examples of this type of plant are grown worldwide every year for this purpose. They can also be used in mass bedding schemes on banks and slopes, planted with their growing points pinched out, so that in a short while the plants will meet up to give a mass effect. This is very helpful in countries where high humidity affects zonal pelargoniums with attacks of rust, as Ivy-Leaf pelargoniums are immune to this problem and can be used instead of zonals for bedding purposes.

'April Hamilton'
Double bright cerise-pink flower

'Abele Carriere'
Semi-double light purple flower, darker feathering

'Amethyst'
Double mauve-purple flower, darker feathering

'Anne'
Double bright mid-purple flower

'Antoinette Crozy'
Semi-double purple flower, large white blaze
in centre

'Barbara Wirth'
Double cerise-pink flower

'Audrey Clifton'
Double coral-scarlet flower

'Barbe Bleue'
Double purple-black flower

'Beatrice Cottington'
Double purple flower

'Beauty of Castlehill'
Double salmon-coral flower

'Beauty of Jersey'
Double cerise-pink flower

'Bella Notte'
Double cerise-crimson flower

'Butterflies'
Single mauve broad-petalled flower lying
closely to the leaf

'Can-Can'
Semi-double coral-pink flower

'Cascade Pink'
Single salmon-pink flower. Mass bloomer

'Cascade Lilac'
Single light lilac flower. Mass bloomer

'Cascade Red'
Single red flower. Mass bloomer

'Cerise Carnation'
Cerise-pink flower, serrated petals

'Col. Baden Powell'
Semi-double blushed pink flower, feathered maroon

'Cornell'
Semi-double bright mauve flower, darker
feathering

'Crocodile'
Semi-double pale coral flower with green and
cream fine cobweb-marked leaf

'Dr Chippault'
Double salmon-rose flower

'Eclipse'
Semi-double rose-pink flower

'Eileen'
Semi-double purple-cerise flower

'Galilee'
Double rose-salmon flower

'Giroflee'
Double deep purple flower

'Golden Lilac Gem'
Double lavender flower with gold leaf

'Harlequin Alpine Glow'
Double carmine-purple and white flower

'Harlequin Liverbird'
Semi-double salmon-red flower, striped white

'Harlequin My Love'
Double light red and white flower, bi-colour

'Harlequin Mahogany'
Double dark red and white flower, bi-colour

'Harlequin Picotee'
Double white flower, edged crimson

'Harlequin Rosie O'Day'
Semi-double pink and white flower

'Harvard'
Semi-double deep red flower

'Hederinum Variegatum'
Single pink flower, variegated cream and green leaf

'Helena'
Double salmon-pink flower

'Icing Sugar'
Double small pale pink flower

'Isidel'
Double cerise-pink flower, centre flushed coral

'Jackie'
Double pale lavender-pink flower

'Joan of Arc'
Semi-double good white flower, wine feathering

'Joker'
Double mauve–purple flower, splashed white

'Lachskonigen'
Semi-double rosy salmon–pink flower

'La France'
Semi-double mauve flower

'L'elegante'
Single palest mauve flower with variegated silver leaf which turns to mauve edge in dry conditions

'Leopard'
Semi-double mauve-pink flower, spotted purple

'Lilac Gem'
Double pale lavender flower

'Lulu'
Double plum-red flower

'Mexican Beauty'
Semi-double light crimson-purple flower

'Mauve Beauty'
Double deep mauve flower, very free flowering

'Mme Crousse'
Semi-double pale pink flower, veined

'Mosaic Red Cascade'
Single red flower, narrow-petalled with
cobweb leaf

'Mosaic Sugar Baby'
Semi-double very small, pale pink-cerise
flower, veined leaf

'Mrs Martin'
Double lavender-pink flower

PAC 'Acapulco'
Single rose-pink flower, white eye

PAC 'Tomcat'
Semi-double deep crimson-black flower

'Mrs W. A. R. Clifton'
Semi-double red flower

'Nels Pierson'
Semi-double lavender-pink flower, dashed wine

'Philiomel'
Semi-double orange-scarlet flower

'Pink Gay Baby'
Double bright pink flower

'Pink Rosebud'
Double soft pink flower

'Purple Prince'
Double purple flower, rosebud-type

'Raviro'
Double cerise-pink flower

'Red Duke'
Single red flower, silver variegated leaf

'Rhodamant'
Double purple flower

'Rigi'
Semi-double cerise-pink flower

'Rosais'
Semi-double bright purple flower

'Rio Grande'
Double almost-black flower with pale reverse

'Rouletta'
Semi-double white flower, edged and striped
red

'Sandra Lorraine'
Double crimson flower, white underneath,
rosebud type

'Sir Arthur Hort'
Single large flower, rose-pink

'Surcouf'
Single wine-red flower

'Snow Queen'
Semi-double white flower, feathered purple

'Solidor'
Semi-double mid-pink flower, early bloomer

'Sybil Holmes'
Double deep pink flower

'Tavira'
Semi-double light cerise-red flower, feathered

'Ville de Paris'
Single rose-salmon flower, profusely flowered

'Veronica Ann'
Semi-double bright scarlet flower, feathered

'Wood's Surprise'
Semi-double soft mauve flower with white
and green marbled leaf

'Yale'
Semi-double blood-red flower, feathered

'White Mesh'
Semi-double pale pink flower with cobweb-marked leaf

HAZEL'S FAVOURITES

My favourite pelargoniums are largely to be found amongst the species. This might seem unusual when there are so many different beautiful cultivars available, but I think the species help to show off the cultivars when combined with a display in a glasshouse. They can be given similar growing conditions too. All the species are available from certain specialist nurseries. Write to the National Pelargonium Collection who can advise you on the nearest location for these. Enclose an s.a.e. with your enquiry.

If you would like more detailed information about species pelargoniums, B.T. Batsford have published a book by Diane Miller entitled *Pelargoniums: A Gardener's Guide to the Species and their Herbs and Cultivars*. It is packed full of information and pictures on this subject.

P. abrotanifolium
Upright stems, narrow pleasant-smelling leaves clustered all the way up the stems

P. appendiculatum
Tuberous cultivar with a deep cream to yellow flower, and grey-green fern-like leaf

P. cortusifolium
Grey-green round leaves on upright stem. Small pink flowers with dots on petals

P. australe
Small-leafed, makes a good pot plant. Small white flowers grow just above foliage

P. odoratissimum
Low growing prostrate shrub of grey-green
leaves and white flowers

P. exstipulatum
Leaves are greyish-green and the flower palest
pink to white

P. fulgidum
A short shrubby plant with grey-green foliage,
oblong cordate leaves and scarlet flowers

P. reniforme
The leaves are reniform and cordate with
crenate margins and are grey-green in colour

P. frutetorum
Narrow-zoned green leaves with profuse
blooming primitive salmon flowers

P. gibbosum
Succulent stemmed plant with swollen joints.
Stems are very brittle

P. klinghardtense
Grey-green succluent foliage and stems with
white flowers

P. lanceolatum
Upright branched plant, woody base
lanceolate grey-green undivided leaves

P. tetragonum
Succulent stems in a bushy habit with sweet-smelling pale mauve flowers

P. ovale
Grey-green low-growing half shrub with leaf blades on long petioles

P. papilionaceum
A good conservatory plant, this vigorous shrub has large mauve clusters of flowers

P. peltatum
Pale mauve flower; green leaves with a small zone in centre

P. rapaceum
Tuberous plant with fertile foliage and flowers appearing on long stems in clusters

P. triste
Geophyte with umbels of yellow and black flowers that are sweetly-scented at night

P. zonal pelargonium
Round, green semi succulent leaves with prominent zones and mauve flowers

***P. cucullatum* subsp.** *strigifolium*
Vigorous-growing shrub with angular leaves and purple flowers

***P. cucullatum* subsp.** *cucullatum*
Cupped rounded leaves with clusters of mauve flowers

P. sidoides
A good plant for a hanging pot, unusual foliage growing on upright leaf stems

P. incrassatum
Geophyte with silvery-green leaves and bright magenta flowers

P. endlicherianum
Difficult to grow outdoors, but grows well in a cold glasshouse

PELARGONIUM AND GERANIUM SOCIETIES

INTERNATIONAL GERANIUM SOCIETY

P.O. Box 92734
Pasadena
C.A. 91109-2734
USA

AUSTRALIAN GERANIUM SOCIETY

Membership Secretary:
Mrs A. Henderson
27 Chichester Street
Maroubra
New South Wales 2035
Australia

BELGIAN PELARGOIUM & GERANIUM SOCIETY

St. Ja Straat 914
3583 Paal-Beringen
Belgium

BRITISH PELARGONIUM AND GERANIUM SOCIETY

Hon. Secretary:
Mr Les Hodgkins
75 Pelham Road
Bexleyheath
Kent
DA7 4LY

THE BRITISH & EUROPEAN GERANIUM SOCIETY

Hon. Secretary:
Mr Richard Hampshire
1 Bishopsteighton
Shoeburyness
Essex
SS3 8AD

GERANIUM & PELARGONIUM SOCIETY OF ONTARIO, CANADA

Membership Chair:
Don & Isabel Piggott
29 Hills Road
AJAX
Ontario
Canada

ITALIAN PELARGONIUM SOCIETY

Secretary:
Raffetti & F. Baldacchino
Via degli Imbriani, 30
20158 Milano
Italy

PELARGONIUM COLLECTIONS

FIBREX NURSERIES

Honeybourne Road
Pebworth
Stratford-Upon-Avon
Warwickshire
CV37 8XP

All types of Pelargonium on display

May, June, July: open Monday to
Friday 10.30 a.m. to 5.00 p.m.
Saturday/Sunday/bank holidays
12.00 noon to 5.00 p.m.
August: open Monday to Friday
10.30 a.m. to 5.00 p.m. Closed
Saturdays & Sundays.

NATIONAL PELARGONIUM COLLECTION (ANGEL)

D.L. Dean
8 Lynwood Close
South Harrow
Middlesex

Open by appointment only.

NATIONAL PELARGONIUM COLLECTION (SUCCULENT SPECIES)

Sydney G. Reed
19 Leyson Road
The Reddings
Cheltenham
Gloucestershire
GL51 6RU

Open by appointment only.